ROMAN LIFE
IN
BRITAIN

Written by Ciaran Murtagh
Illustrated by Rudolf Farkas

CONTENTS

D1610808

Collins

WHO WERE THE CELTS?

The time before the Romans **invaded** Britain is known as the Iron Age (800 BCE–43 CE). The people who lived in Britain at that time were called the Celts. The Celts were divided into lots of different **tribes**, each with a different king or queen. Sometimes these tribes would argue and fight.

a Celtic village

The Celts lived in small villages. Their houses were made of wattle and daub (branches and mud) and sometimes farmyard animals lived inside with them.

It made counting sheep at bedtime much easier!

Celtic clothes

woollen cloak

linen tunic

leather shoes

trousers

skirt

3

WHO WERE THE ROMANS?

Romans originally came from the city of Rome in Italy. By the time they invaded Britain in 43 CE, they ruled a large **empire** made up of millions of people. The Romans were led by an emperor and they had a powerful army.

DID YOU KNOW?

The first ruler of Rome was called Romulus, and legend has it he was raised by a wolf!

Romulus and his brother Remus with their wolf mother

The emperor used the army to **conquer** new lands. Once a new land had been conquered, the people living there had to pay money to Rome. This is how Rome became rich and powerful.

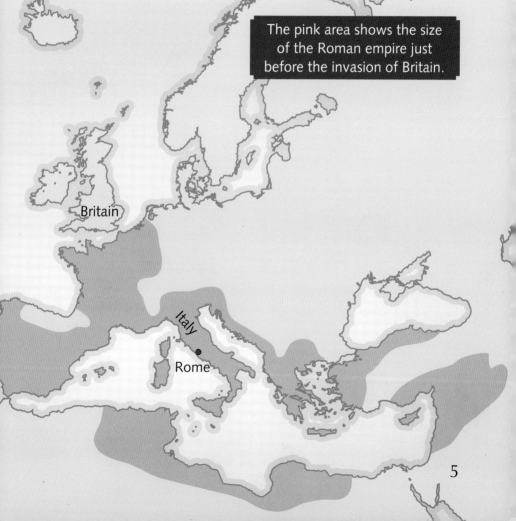

The pink area shows the size of the Roman empire just before the invasion of Britain.

Britain

Italy

Rome

WHY DID THE ROMANS INVADE BRITAIN?

By 43 CE, Rome had a new emperor called Claudius. Other emperors had tried to conquer Britain before, but had failed. Claudius decided to prove he was a strong leader by being the first emperor to conquer Britain.

Claudius believed that Britain was a rich country with lots of gold and silver mines. He wanted some of that wealth for the empire.

DID YOU KNOW?
Claudius's full name was Tiberius Claudius Caesar Augustus Germanicus. What a tongue twister!

Mine! All mine!

purple cloak

toga – the purple border showed that Claudius was important

THE INVASION

Claudius invaded Britain in 43 CE. He brought 40,000 troops with him. He even had war elephants.

Roman soldiers riding a war elephant

The Roman army was very good at fighting. They were well trained and had the best weapons available. Because the Celts came from different tribes, they disagreed about what to do when the Roman invasion started. Some wanted to fight; others wanted to **surrender**. Celts who didn't surrender thought they would be safe in their hill forts.

Claudius's army burnt many hill forts to the ground. Four months after he arrived, Claudius claimed Britain as part of the empire.

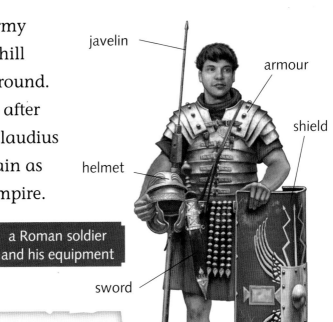

javelin

armour

shield

helmet

sword

a Roman soldier and his equipment

DID YOU KNOW?
Roman soldiers marched up to 30 kilometres per day, carrying everything they needed with them.

a Celtic hill fort

THE RESISTANCE

Some of the Celtic leaders didn't like being ruled from Rome. They didn't want to have their lands taken or to pay money to Rome. They fought back. One leader, Caractacus, led sneaky attacks against the Romans. Another, Boudicca, used an army of thousands to attack Roman towns. Both were stopped by the powerful Roman army.

Even though Emperor Claudius claimed victory in 43 CE, it took over 30 years for some parts of Britain to come under Roman rule. Even then, parts of Scotland were never conquered.

11

ROMAN TOWNS

Celts lived in small villages in the countryside.
Romans liked to live in towns. After the invasion, they
built towns all over Britain. Roman towns were always
built in the same way, with streets laid out in a grid.
At the centre of the town was a market place known
as the forum. The town hall, or basilica, was next to
the market place.

Many Roman towns were surrounded by a wall to keep them safe. Most towns had baths where you could wash, and bigger towns had an **amphitheatre** where people could watch sports.

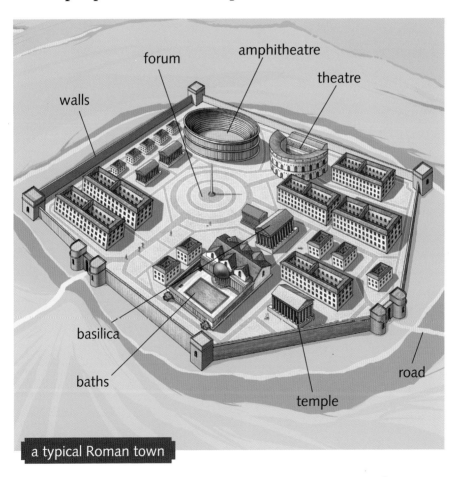

a typical Roman town

Roman remains

Romans built their towns out of bricks and stone. This meant they lasted well, and you can still see some Roman ruins today. One of the best preserved Roman ruins is in Caerwent, Wales. Under the Romans, Caerwent was known as *Venta Silurum*, and it became the biggest town in Wales.

Historians think that up to 3,000 people lived there. Caerwent had an amphitheatre, a public baths and walls over five metres high, which modern visitors can still see.

Caerwent then …

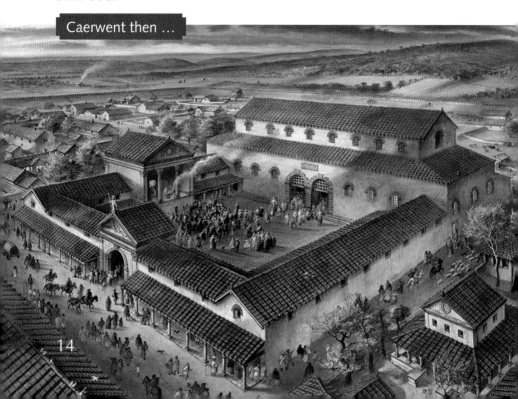

14

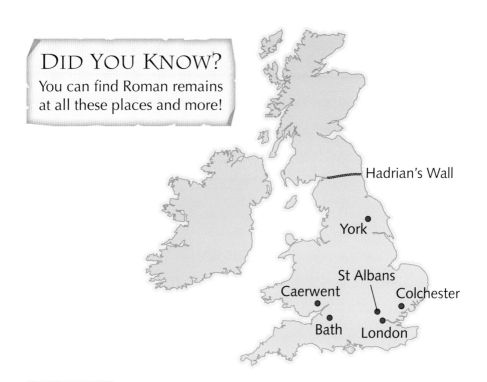

Hadrian's Wall

York

St Albans

Caerwent

Colchester

Bath   London

... and now

ROMAN HOMES

In Roman Britain, the type of house you lived in depended on how rich or important you were. Rich Romans lived in large town houses made of brick and stone. They had many rooms. Large houses might have a small **temple** and their own bathroom, and they were often decorated with colourful **mosaics**.

Only five thousand, nine hundred and seventy-nine pieces to go.

a mosaic of a dolphin found at Bignor Roman **villa** in Sussex

a modern copy of a
Roman villa at Wroxeter

Poorer Romans lived in
smaller houses made of
stone, wood and mud.
Shopkeepers and their
families often lived in
rooms above their shop.

DID YOU KNOW?

The Romans even had
central heating! It was called
a hypocaust system and was
specially built so that hot air
from a **furnace** could flow
under the floors, heating
them up.

TRANSPORT

With so many towns popping up all over
Britain, the Romans built roads to connect them.
Before the Romans arrived, the Celts used muddy
tracks to get from
place to place.
This wasn't a fast
way to get around.
The Romans built
long roads so that
they could get from
place to place quickly.

Not more roadworks!

how Roman roads
were built

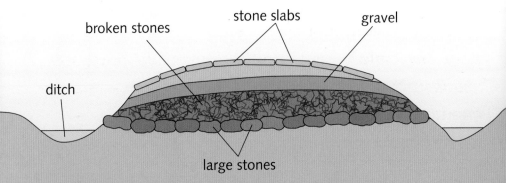

broken stones

stone slabs

gravel

ditch

large stones

DID YOU KNOW?
The Romans built about 16,000
kilometres of road in Britain!

part of the Roman road over
Wheeldale Moor in North Yorkshire

Fast roads meant that goods could be transported,
messages could be sent and the army could march to
wherever they were needed. Roman roads were usually
about two and a half metres wide and made of stone.
They were also known for being very straight.

19

FOOD

Before the Romans arrived, the Celts mainly ate bread, stew and porridge.

But the Romans brought all sorts of new foods with them, which they began to grow in Britain.

Celtic cooking

food growing in a Roman garden

DID YOU KNOW?

Romans had a recipe for stuffed dormouse – eek! Or should that be squeak!?

As well as new foods, the Romans introduced new ways of eating too. The main meal of the day was called "cena", and it happened late in the afternoon. Romans would wash before every meal and lie on couches eating with their fingers. It was like a TV dinner without the TV!

That's what I call fast food!

NEW ROMAN FOODS

- ◆ rabbits
- ◆ cucumbers
- ◆ peas
- ◆ carrots
- ◆ cabbage
- ◆ lettuce
- ◆ onion

It had never been easier to eat your vegetables!

"cena" time for a Roman family

Fashion

Roman Britons liked to be trendy! What you wore depended on how rich and important you were. Slaves and ordinary people wore simple tunics fastened with a belt. However, powerful and important Romans liked to wear fine fabrics and expensive jewellery.

Roman men (and sometimes women) wore a garment called a "toga", which was difficult to put on and very heavy. If you were really important, you were allowed to put a purple band on your toga.

WHY DID THEY LEAVE?

About 400 years after they arrived, the Romans left Britain. Other parts of the empire were being attacked and soldiers were needed to go and defend them. The Roman Empire was getting weaker and other empires were getting stronger.

a Roman quinquereme ship leaving Britain

By 410 CE, Emperor Honorius announced that
the people of Britain had to look after themselves.
The Romans had gone.

Without Roman soldiers, Britain was left open
to attack. Soon Angles, Saxons and Jutes
began to invade from northern Europe.
We call these invaders
the Anglo-Saxons.

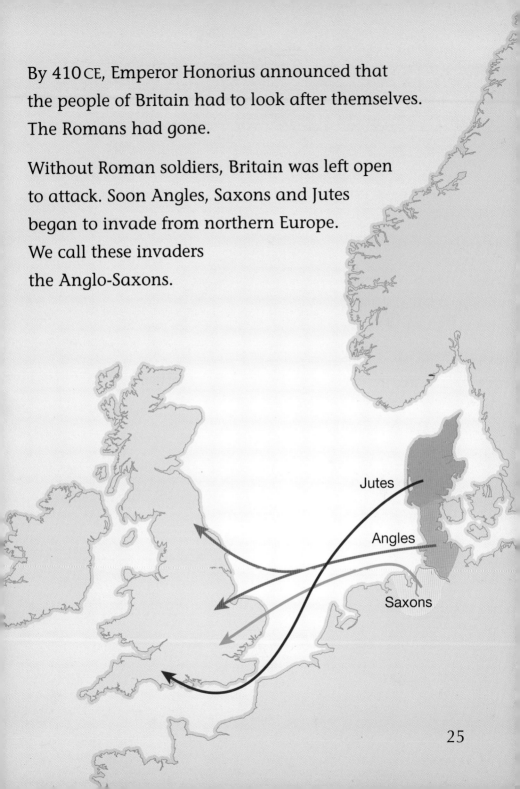

Jutes

Angles

Saxons

WHAT DID THE ROMANS LEAVE BEHIND?

Even though the Romans had gone, they left a lot of things behind that we still use to this day. Some of our roads are built on top of ancient Roman roads.

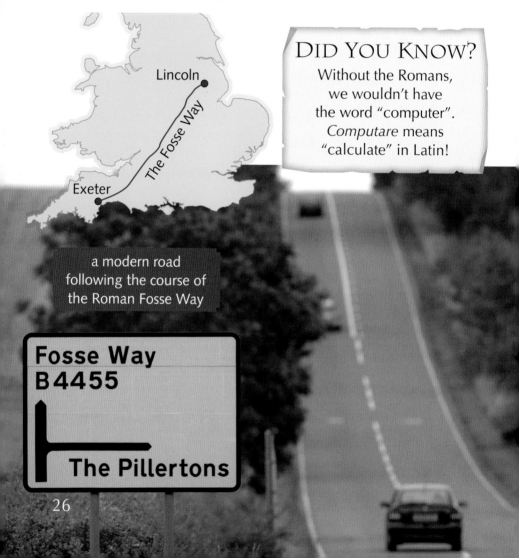

Lincoln

The Fosse Way

Exeter

DID YOU KNOW?

Without the Romans, we wouldn't have the word "computer". *Computare* means "calculate" in Latin!

a modern road following the course of the Roman Fosse Way

Fosse Way
B4455

The Pillertons

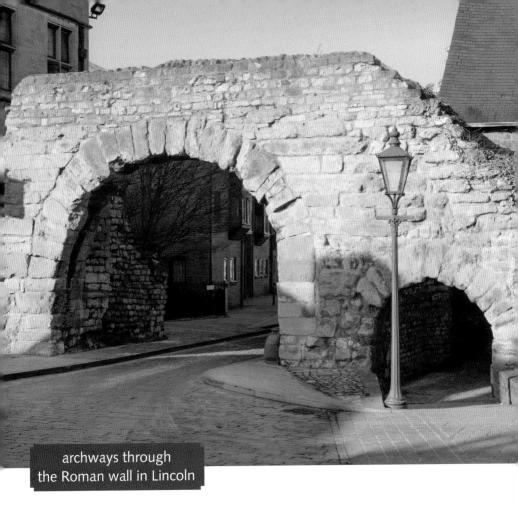

archways through
the Roman wall in Lincoln

Some towns in Britain still have parts of their **original** Roman walls.

Many common English words (like "entrance", "exit", "long", "famous") come from the Latin language spoken by the Romans. Even the planets in our solar system were named after Roman gods like Mercury, Venus and Neptune!

GLOSSARY

amphitheatre	an oval or round building with seats rising in rows from a central area
conquer	defeat
empire	a group of countries that is ruled by one country
furnace	a place where a fire can be lit, a bit like an oven
invaded	entered by force
mosaics	pictures made out of tiny stones
original	real, unaltered
surrender	give in
temple	a building where people worship their god or gods
tribes	groups of people who live together, with each tribe having their own leader
villa	a large house

INDEX

THE ROMANS INVADE BRITAIN

4 **78 CE**
The Romans conquer Wales.

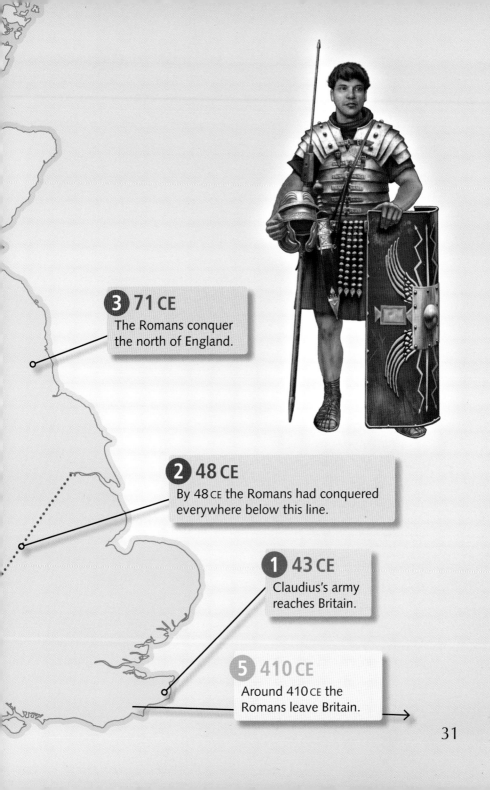

3 **71 CE**

The Romans conquer the north of England.

2 **48 CE**

By 48 CE the Romans had conquered everywhere below this line.

1 **43 CE**

Claudius's army reaches Britain.

5 **410 CE**

Around 410 CE the Romans leave Britain.

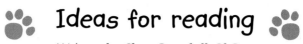

Ideas for reading

Written by Clare Dowdall, PhD
Lecturer and Primary Literacy Consultant

Reading objectives:
- read books that are structured in different ways
- discuss their understanding and explain the meaning of words in context
- ask questions to improve understanding

Spoken language objectives:
- use spoken language to develop understanding through speculating, hypothesising, imagining and exploring ideas

Curriculum links: History – Roman Empire

Resources: ICT, pens and paper, outline of Britain.

Build a context for reading

- Ask children what they know about the Romans and Roman life in Britain. Create a rough timeline to show the year 0, 43 CE (invasion), and today to give a sense of the timescale covered.
- Look at the front cover together. Discuss what the child is doing and what is happening in the illustration.
- Turn to the blurb and read it aloud to the children. Ask children to suggest why the Romans might have travelled to Britain originally, and why they left.

Understand and apply reading strategies

- Turn to the contents. Discuss how the book is organised (by timeline and by theme).
- Ask children what they think "resistance" means. Prompt them to use contextual and word-level information to predict an answer, e.g. it must be related to "invasion" as it follows it in the chapter headings; it has the word "resist" in it, which means to fight against.